Repeat After Me

Simple Truths to Help You
Survive a Crisis

Kathryn D. Adis

BALBOA.
PRESS

A DIVISION OF HAY HOUSE

Balboa Press books may be ordered through booksellers or by contacting:

Balboa Press
A Division of Hay House
1663 Liberty Drive
Bloomington, IN 47403
www.balboapress.com
1 (877) 407-4847

Because of the dynamic nature of the Internet, any web addresses or links contained in this book may have changed since publication and may no longer be valid. The views expressed in this work are solely those of the author and do not necessarily reflect the views of the publisher, and the publisher hereby disclaims any responsibility for them.

The author of this book does not dispense medical advice or prescribe the use of any technique as a form of treatment for physical, emotional, or medical problems without the advice of a physician, either directly or indirectly. The intent of the author is only to offer information of a general nature to help you in your quest for emotional and spiritual well-being. In the event you use any of the information in this book for yourself, which is your constitutional right, the author and the publisher assume no responsibility for your actions.

Any people depicted in stock imagery provided by Thinkstock are models, and such images are being used for illustrative purposes only.
Certain stock imagery © Thinkstock.

Print information available on the last page.

ISBN: 978-1-5043-8143-7 (sc)
ISBN: 978-1-5043-8144-4 (e)

Library of Congress Control Number: 2017908716

Balboa Press rev. date: 09/11/2017

Dedication

I dedicate this book to a tender man who is unaware of the impact he makes on the life of every person who crosses his path. Don, the universe was looking out for me when you came into my life. I love you.

I also dedicate this book to my son who loved me back into health with his unassuming, gentle ways. Justin, you have always celebrated my tentative steps of growth. I love you simply for being in my life.

Tara, Jake Andrew, and Taylor Olivia Adis, you are angels of love and light on my path.

I am so grateful to my family members and precious friends who selflessly set aside time to care for me. I turned to each of you for comfort and encouragement and always found what I needed. In particular, thank you Linda Dean, T. Caylor Wadlington, Karon Buckner Scott, Kris Johnson, Rita Pech, Georgia and Bob Torson, Su Dierbeck, Chris Dierbeck, Lynn Scott, Kathy Dietz, Leigh and Anne Dierbeck, John and Mary Dierbeck, Kathleen Dietz, Cindy Skalicky, Musette Young, and Betty Milan.

Above all else, I am grateful to The All for gentle and not-so-gentle nudges along the way.

Be ground.
Be crumbled,
So wildflowers will come up where you are.
You've been stony for too many years.
Try something different.
Surrender.
Rumi

Contents

Foreword

July 28, 2002, was a beautiful summer day in Colorado with clear skies and eighty-degree temperatures. The interstate was crowded with traffic at the end of a busy weekend on the Front Range. In fact, the southbound lanes were stopped completely, and our car was the last in a line of stalled traffic.

With no warning, an RV traveling at an estimated speed of seventy miles per hour slammed into the back of our stalled car, caroming us into three other vehicles. Every panel of our car was demolished, leaving the vehicle unrecognizable. My wife and I were rendered unconscious.

At the moment of the collision, a state trooper who had been cruising northbound, witnessed the impact and sent out a call for the local fire and rescue department. The fire and rescue squad was the first on the scene and called for assistance from a Flight for Life crew. Realizing the severity of Kathy's injuries, a paramedic climbed under the tarp and stabilized her spinal column while the team cut off the roof of our car so they could extricate us.

Shortly thereafter, the helicopter landed, and within minutes Kathy was whisked away. I was taken by ambulance to a nearby hospital where my injuries were determined to be incredibly minor. Kathy had not been so lucky. She suffered a usually fatal fractured second cervical (C2) vertebra, known as the "hangman's fracture" in the medical profession. This injury, along with severe trauma to the back of her skull, affected her vision, her vocal cords, and her ability to swallow.

The emergency room staff fitted her with a halo, a device consisting of a hard, plastic harness from waist to shoulders, attached to four metal rods. The top of the halo was attached with steel screws at four points around the circumference of her skull. Miraculously, no nerve damage occurred, and the medical staff was stunned. They called Kathy "the miracle lady."

During the following month in the hospital, Kathy was nourished with a feeding tube through her abdomen. She was in incredible pain, and it took almost three weeks of trial and error to find a proper mixture of medications. In the process, she lost twenty-five pounds.

After twenty-eight days, Kathy was discharged, still sporting the halo and receiving nourishment through the feeding tube. What followed were six weeks of twenty-four-hour home care, more and different medications, trips to psychologists and psychiatrists to address her depression and suicidal thoughts, and visits by occupational therapist and nutritionists.

Finally, after almost three months, the halo came off and the feeding tube came out. Within five months, she weaned herself off medications and began the long road to physical, mental, and spiritual recovery.

The years that have passed since the collision have made me a witness to the physical and spiritual rebirth of the person

I have loved for over forty-five years. She has brought many wonderful people into her life during the process who have helped her find the keys to unlock her personal journey through life in a very special and inspiring way. Her challenges have awakened the desire in me to repeat after her. So too, they may do the same for you.

This is the story of her journey.

Don Adis

An Invitation

While I was assisting in my mother's healing process, one thing became very clear to me: regardless of the number of people who surrounded her with love and attention, at the end of the day, she was alone. Nobody could force her to feel better or heal more quickly. My father sat at her side every single day. Every hour of every day, loved ones were there to support her. While that surely helped, the ultimate healing power came from within her. It was her decision to live and thrive that pulled her through.

After seeing first hand the unbelievable progress my mother made, I have come to believe that we are what we think. So, it's to our benefit to surround ourselves with people and ideas that inspire us to feel and think positively and passionately about our lives, health, and choices.

Take to heart the ideas and thoughts written by my mother. She is more than qualified to write this book, and she does so with the hope of inspiring you and others to see the light at the end of any dark tunnel.

Justin Adis

Preface

*For, while the tale of how we suffer, and how we are
delighted, and how we may triumph is never new, it
always must be heard. There isn't any other tale to
tell, it's the only light we've got in all this darkness.*
James Baldwin, "Sonny's Blues"

Are you facing a difficult time right now? Do you feel as though
you've been slammed into an experience that has left you
confused, angry, hurt, or frightened? Perhaps the mundane
routines of life have been swept out from under you and a new
reality and unknown future is facing you. Your experience
may be more difficult than mine, or perhaps may not seem as
significant. This is of no consequence. These simple truths
can be your North Star, a leaning post, a benevolent escort
into a new, expanded, empowered next season of your life.

Try out some of the thoughts I present and determine for
yourself if they feel good to you. Hang on to the concepts that
resonate inside your body. What doesn't resonate with you,
toss overboard.

Ready? Take a deep breath now. Open your heart. Let the
inspiration given me as I healed and wrote *Repeat After Me*
provide you the first step on the path to a joyous, new you.

Simple Truth Number 1

When one door closes, another opens.

> *There is no ending without a beginning. Beginnings*
> *and endings are always right up against each other.*
> Rachel Naomi Remen[1]

This truth is much easier to accept when the door is slamming on someone else. And yet, this is the first simple truth I ask you to believe: when one door closes, another opens.

Many doors closed in and around me on July 28, 2002. My body became a stranger, no longer able to function at will. Self-reliance, my barometer of maturity and ego-identity, disappeared as I found myself at the mercy of medical staff, tubes, machines, and caregivers. After a lifetime of being a giver, I became the receiver, dependent on family members, friends, and strangers for my survival.

While I was suffering pain, disorientation, insomnia, and crippling fear and depression, life looked horrendous, even though I couldn't turn my neck to see it. People continued

---

[1]   Rachel Naomi Reman, *Kitchen Table Wisdom* (Penguin Group USA, Inc. 2006).

to assure me that I would get better. "You're a fighter. You'll be better in no time," they insisted. "Easy for you to say," I mumbled in response. I would never be the same again, and frankly, I had neither the energy nor the faith to envision a new reality, much less hope it would be bearable.

One by one, the doctors released me from their care long before I felt ready. I wanted to scream, "How dare you tell me there's nothing more you can do! Who's going to fix me?" Fragile, despondent, and dependent upon others for transportation and activities within and outside the home, I turned to my physical therapist for support and encouragement. Three days a week for six months I became a model client, believing exercise was the key to my recovery, certain that healing was all about making my body whole again. (I had a lot to learn.) My physical therapy sessions became an emotional lifeline in my endless, fear-filled days. The staff gently supported and comforted me through my depression and tears, and most importantly, held the beacon of hope high when I could not. Eventually, though, even that door slammed in my face when I was told that the insurance company would not longer support that treatment. I was set adrift, and the emotional downslide continued.

Ever so slowly, I began to realize that I could rely on yet another door. It was a ray of hope, be it a new perspective, a different method of self-care or relief in some unexpected form. I came to know to my core and without a shadow of a doubt that everything *always* works out for me, then I watched for evidence of that belief every day. Any fear I was feeling revealed itself to me as fear of an unknown future, and a fear that I would never get better. I learned to simply surrender to the pain and the anxiety, and then take the next step, whatever revealed itself to me as a possible source of hope. I scheduled that appointment, got that book, or listened to that inspiration. Relief always came.

Yes, my body operates differently today, but I cherish it more and scrutinize it less.

Yes, relationships changed or ended as I learned to take care of myself *first*, but self-love has deepened my love for others.

Yes, on July 28, 2002, my life changed forever. But today I can clearly reflect on the absolute perfection of every moment along the way. The physical journey has been lengthy and challenging, and it continues even today, but the true healing has been a path built upon the cobblestones of self-discovery and spiritual awareness, bringing me to a state of empowerment and fearlessness about whatever arises.

As you experience doors closing and opening during a time of challenge, I invite you to consider the following as your companions in the midst of your transition between endings and beginnings:

Your breath is your connection to life. Sit in a quiet, safe space once a day and allow the life-giving energy that is carried on your breath to move through your body. The breath, not the brain, connects us to the body's innate ability to process and heal emotionally and physically. You can tap into this magnificent healing power with focused breathing a few moments each day.

Write down your thoughts along the way. Your own record of your emotions, reflections, and evolving understandings of your situation will become a barometer of your healing, enabling you to look back in wonder at your progress.

Remain unattached to the outcome. You'll experience uncertainty during this time of transition. Your tendency will be to attach to a predetermined outcome. I encourage you to let go of all expectations. Your most valuable work is to foster an observer's mind and surrender to what presents itself physically or emotionally. As Matt Kahn encourages, "whatever arises, love that."[2] This means, if a good feeling arises, bask in it for as long as you can; if a negative thought or feeling arises, gift yourself with the kind of compassion you would gift another. You don't have to like what you're going through or feeling. You may not understand why you're going through whatever it is. You can certainly "piss and moan with perspective," tweets Dr. Brené Brown, research professor at the University of Houston Graduate College of Social Work. But then shower yourself with loving self-reassurances and move on.

Pay attention to surprise encounters and unexpected experiences. Dare to trust your own intuition by paying attention to the impulses and seeming synchronicities you might otherwise ignore. A song may inspire you. A friend may appear at just the right time to renew your hope. Books will cross your table, and clarity will seem to come out of the blue. My library is filled with books that friends suggested. Some I've read from cover to cover, and others I began but didn't finish. Every author

---

[2]   Matt Kahn, *Whatever Arises, Love That* (Sounds True, Boulder, CO, 2016).

presented messages I could wrap my brain and my heart around. I've listed a few at the end of this book.

Ask for support from your friends. In the process of giving to you, your friends and caregivers will feel good about themselves. When they pray for you, they pray for themselves. When they encourage you to hang in there, they encourage themselves. As they watch you, you are giving them a template for healing to be called upon when they face their own challenges. We need one another.

When a dear friend assured me that doors were opening, I trusted her because she had survived a broken back while she was a single mother caring for three young boys. Today she manifests courage, integrity, and serenity. She is living proof that good can come out of tragedy. When she spoke, I listened.

Now repeat after me: *When one door closes, another opens.* And so it does.

Simple Truth Number 2

Words and thoughts create your reality.

We are the product of our prevailing habits of thought.
Venice J. Bloodworth, PhD[3]

We get the impression from our society that we are in control. Yet despite the time and energy we have expended in maintaining this charade, life can suddenly be filled with chaos, leaving us feeling vulnerable and powerless.

Before the *collision*[4], my body moved with ease and grace. When it was time to dress, I dressed. When it was time to care for my family, there was no question that I could handle my obligations. When it was time to exercise or hike or bike or golf or ski, I implicitly trusted my body to respond, taking for granted all my mental and physical capabilities—until the impact. Then the scaffolding crumbled beneath my feet.

---

[3]   Venice J. Bloodworth, *Key to Yourself: Opening the Door to a Joyful Life from Within* (DeVorss & Company, 1979).

[4]   A friend suggested that I use the word *impact* or *collision* instead of *accident*. I took her suggestion because I have learned that there are no accidents in life; there are no victims.

In an instant, I couldn't walk, swallow, or feed myself. I couldn't be left alone, bathe myself, dress myself, or tend to my most basic needs. I couldn't hug anyone because of the halo. I couldn't sit or lie comfortably. I couldn't distract myself by reading, staring off into the distance, or watching television because my vision doubled from the impact. I couldn't get in my car and flee from reality for the same reason. I had to be my own entertainment, and it felt like hell on earth.

Silence frightened me. Always a doer and an achiever, sitting still unnerved me. I didn't know how to be alone with myself. As I lost the ability to do familiar, comforting, and distracting activities, terror filled my mind; I found myself in a very dark emotional tunnel. For weeks on end I grappled with the staggering choice of ending my life or hanging on by my fingernails. Only my reluctance to cause more pain for my family stopped me from committing suicide.

One morning, after months of physical healing and ongoing emotional chaos, I awoke with a certainty flooding my brain: *I don't have to be a victim!* Although I proclaimed it aloud to my husband, this new perspective wavered in the months ahead. And yet, the life-altering moment shifted my awareness. If I was to survive, I had to stop playing a victim and discover a new source of control and understanding, one more enduring and reliable than my pre-collision illusions.

Time marched on, and the healing continued. Almost two years later, when a caring friend asked how I was feeling, I blurted out "Great!"—only to look around in disbelief at hearing such a positive comment come out of my mouth. I certainly wasn't great. I was still seeing double, my skull ached, and my neck rotation was limited. What had prompted me to say I felt great, I wondered?

My reality was shifting. With that simple word—*great*—I experienced a palpable sense of mastery over the moment. The effect was so profound that I became a strict guardian of my words. Quickly, I noticed that when I spoke only words that lifted me up, words that came from a wellspring of self-love, I hurt less, or the discomfort lessened. The aches and pains felt manageable and temporary. And if you have only the capacity to utter "I love you" to yourself, you are washing your body with a powerful healing energy.

The Serenity Prayer can help you reframe your thoughts and keep you on track. Allow it to support you: *God, grant me the serenity to accept the things I cannot change, courage to change the things I can, and wisdom to know the difference.*[5]

Let go of what you *can't* change. The collision, divorce, diagnosis, or event happened. It can't be reversed. Your body, job, marriage, or life will never be the same again. Let go of the illusion that you can rewrite the story. It can be that easy.

Change the things you *can* change at each moment, beginning with your thoughts and words. Practice responding differently when you're asked how you feel. Practice shifting your thoughts from "I can't" to "I choose to." Give up the victim role. Be courageous and disciplined about thinking affirming thoughts. No one else can do this for you.

When you face fear, anger, or pain, ask, "What can I control at this moment?" Then choose serenity by accepting what you cannot change and be courageous about changing what you

---

[5]   Written by American theologian Reinhold Niebuhr (1892–1971).

can. Your struggles *will* fade away and your path *will* become clearer and more manageable. It's all in *your* control.

Now repeat after me: *Words and thoughts create my reality.* They do.

Simple Truth Number 3

Your soul is on a perfect journey, and your body is along for the ride.

Every circumstance—no matter how painful—is s
a gauntlet thrown down by the Universe, challenging
us to become who we are capable of being.
Marianne Williamson[6]

Have you ever had an inkling that there is more to life than can be explained by the five senses? Perhaps an inspirational book you read during a difficult time hinted at a divine purpose. Perhaps the suggestion of a friend invited you to consider the deeper meaning to your life. Perhaps the possibility of a power greater than yourself entered your consciousness during a worship service or a support group meeting.

When these notions crept into my awareness, I swept them aside as soon as the difficulty eased or the inspiring words faded from my memory. Yes, I wanted to know that there was more to life than the challenges I experienced, but I

---

6   Marianne Williamson, *The Gift of Change* (New York, HarperCollins, 2004).

was absolutely unwilling to give up the command of my ship to some unknown entity. I longed for comfort, peace, and purpose, yet resisted any belief that sounded like the religious dogma from my youth. I yearned for understanding and faith, but spiritual transformation had to be quick so I could get on with my important life. I craved truth, yet the message had to be delivered loudly and succinctly or I wouldn't hear it over the din of my daily activities. Be careful what you wish for ...

In the middle of another busy day, an angel disguised as a human being driving a large recreational vehicle stopped me. I was brought to the brink of physical death and given the opportunity to try life again. No more having "one toe in the door" to conscious living. No more excuses for putting off the search for meaning to my life. Along with gifts of flowers, cards, and visits, the gift of time to become conscious was laid at my feet. I was unceremoniously stopped in my tracks. The collision wasn't a mistake or an accident—it was my *soul* crying out for attention. (I use the term *soul* to describe that part of us that transcends the physical body. This aspect of our selves has been called by many names, such as Higher Self or Spirit. I invite you to substitute any term that inspires you.)

Physical healing consumed every waking moment of my existence for the first months and even years. It is the same with any crisis or loss. Ever so slowly, however, I refocused my energies to pay attention to my total well-being—body, mind, *and* soul. Some of my friends challenged me to get over it and move on. I agreed that I didn't want to wallow, yet I felt compelled to use the time I'd been given to deeply explore the purpose of the collision within the trajectory of my life, and to understand and accept the perfection of the journey.

If you've been stopped in your tracks, you may notice that your wardrobe, diet, to-do lists, and the latest toy have been drained of importance. The disaster, diagnosis, divorce, or collision is *your soul crying out for your attention.* Use the time you've been given to uncover the precious gifts you hold within.

Healing from any trauma begins when you become aware that life's journey is about more than the physical accoutrements with which we fill our lives. Healing deepens as we take the walk of transformation, awakening to the truth of our existence and purpose on this planet.

We have the gift of choice every single moment. Wallow in self-pity—or thrive. Be a victim—or a survivor. Feel helpless—or feel powerful. We can walk with strength and intention, or hide in fear and smallness. Shoulders squared and heart open—or body bent in protection. What is your choice?

Repeat after me: *My soul is on a perfect journey, and my body is along for the ride.* You are and it is.

Simple Truth Number 4

Your new normal is a boundless journey.

*Universal Spirit is at work peacefully, and
your attempts to rush it or tug new life into full
creative flower will destroy the entire process.*
Dr. Wayne W. Dyer[7]

Long before the impact, I enjoyed the sport of amateur auto racing, a perfect metaphor for my life. My pace was fast, my attention keen, my expectations clear, and my goals defined. I measured a productive day by the number of chores I crossed off my list. I mastered what my mother described as "time-and-motion study": the art of doing at least two things at one time. "Take a load of laundry up the stairs when you go," she would counsel. Employers and friends regularly commented on how quickly I worked and accomplished tasks. I took their words as praise and fine-tuned my talents for their ongoing approval.

---

[7]   Wayne C. Dyer, PhD, *Living the Wisdom of the Tao* (California, Hay House, Inc, 2008).

Focus and race to the finish line on the designated route. This was my MO, my method of operation. The Greek word for this concept of time is *chronos*—quantitative, linear time.

When I was stopped in my tracks, I approached the process of recovery with that *chronos* mindset. My internal clock was set, and once my mind cleared, I was determined to let nothing get in the way of healing. I had things to do, places to go, and an agenda for how to get there. My goal was absolute: get back to normal.

Our results-oriented society supports this mindset. If we don't like something, we throw it out, change channels, or hit the delete button. Zap; it's gone. If we feel sick, we take a pill, and the symptoms ease. If we fall out of love, we get a divorce. Problem solved. If someone treats us wrongfully, we sue. All satisfyingly fast. All about *chronos*.

When the doctors and therapists released me from their care, I felt betrayed and abandoned, confused and alone. I had no sense of direction. I didn't know where to head next or how to start over. The track was unpaved, the turns unpredictable, and the finish line unclear. I felt depleted by rage and despair. The well was empty.

And not a moment too soon.

At last, the multidimensional healing of body, mind, and soul could begin. Where quantitative time had been my enemy, I was now stepping into *kairos*, defined as qualitative time or non-linear time. What does *kairos* look and feel like? Start–learn–grow–heal–meander–learn–grow–heal ... without end, without judgment, and without a timeline.

I've learned to appreciate quiet moments, a slow walk, a good conversation, and the kindness of strangers. I've learned to anticipate and value each moment of every day exactly as it presents itself, surrendering to the journey, relinquishing a false sense of control over my future. My intention has shifted from returning to the old normal to exploring and creating a new persona grounded in a growing spiritual consciousness— all simple to say but requiring discipline. Surrendering to an unknown future is not for the feint of heart.

As you begin this journey, be extremely patient with yourself. Honor the fact that you are in a state of transition. It takes time for a body to heal. It takes time to fashion a new life after loss of any kind. Most importantly, it takes time for one's brain to peel away the layers of old thinking and process a new reality.

My eyesight is a metaphor for this simple truth. Before the collision, I was compulsive about clean glasses and a perfect prescription. I did whatever was necessary to keep my vision clear and precise. Ironically, a long-term physical result of the impact had been double, foggy vision. One day when I was lamenting this change, a friend suggested that I had been given the gift of limited vision to encourage me to close my eyes and look within. So, I did.

The reward? A limitless horizon, an expanded, deeper, and richer world to explore and design to my heart's content.

Although I was filled with rage when my physical therapist suggested I would have to come to grips with a "new normal," she was right. My life would never be the same again. It would be better in ways I couldn't imagine. I now live a truly fearless life. If this sounds good to you, open your mind and heart, and begin to trust the limitless, boundless creativity of every waking moment. Everything is *always* working out for you.

Patience can be a most challenging friend. Life-altering events transform every facet of life, but only time will reveal how deeply and how beautifully. For this moment in time, simply open your heart to whatever presents itself.

Ready? Repeat after me: *My new normal is a boundless journey.* It is.

Simple Truth Number 5

You are in charge of your healing.

Our deepest fear is not that are we inadequate. Our deepest fear is that we are powerful beyond measure.
Marianne Williamson[8]

I've always been curious. A bit of a rebel in a very traditional family, I was drawn to holistic healers[9] early in life. I could not defend my trust in these practitioners from a scientific or logical standpoint. My faith in the efficacy of out-of-the-box healing options was purely intuitive, the best kind of knowledge.

On July 28, 2002, I was rendered unconscious and had to surrender to the intelligence of the Western medical community: the paramedics, the Flight for Life crew, the emergency room staff, and the hospital staff. My family joined

---

[8]   Marianne Williamson, *A Return to Love* (New York, HarperCollins, 1992).

[9]   I use the term *healer* loosely, understanding that only I have the power to heal myself. Practitioners are there to remind us of our ability and show us avenues that expand our understanding of how powerful we really are.

this partnership of caregivers to make critical decisions for my survival and comfort.

On a conscious level, I was unaware of my situation and surroundings for several weeks. On an unconscious level, my Higher Self was busy taking charge of my healing. While still in the emergency room as I struggled to survive, I evidently called out for the one person I implicitly trusted—a medical intuitive, a friend who can see physical energy blocks within a body that could or have already resulted in disease. We had met several years before the impact, and our relationship had grown into a spiritual partnership. I instinctively knew I would find guidance and comfort from her.

This intuitive response to my needs continued. Although of no specific religious persuasion, I asked the hospital chaplain to come to my bedside and help me meditate. Because my mind was altered from massive doses of medication, I don't remember asking for him, but I clearly remember the feeling of peace when he walked through the door. A doctor of acupuncture, also in my cadre of practitioners prior to the collision, came often to my bedside once I was home. From the beginning, he eased my fears by repeatedly telling me, "You'll heal, Kathy." A gentle man, he unblocked my energy and facilitated a faster mending of the vertebrae. His soul touched mine with his calming words. I relied on his conviction when I had none. These practitioners and several other angels brought their gifts to my bedside. They shared their wisdom with me and were ports in the storm as I emerged from my physical and psychic pain.

Day and night in the hospital, I kept the sounds of soft, meditative/spa music playing through headphones. The music helped me hold a safe space while tuning out the surrounding chaos and noise. Once I was home, music continued to be an important element for creating calm in my environment.

Over the years, as I've chosen a variety of modalities, the subtlety of each has brought another dimension to my healing. When I presumed to predict an outcome, I was consistently and gently reminded that only the journey is in my control. As if to reward my trust, I discovered that, when I remained open-minded about my recovery options and my path to wholeness, just the right people, each with unique skills, found their way into my circle of support. I now have unshakable confidence that the appropriate healer/teacher/angel will come when I am ready for the lesson.

Not long ago, I discovered another level of understanding for this simple truth: You are in charge of your healing. I thought that being open to alternative modalities and choosing the right practitioner was the meaning. Once again, I had more to learn. Being in charge can mean something much deeper—if you choose—because another level of healing occurs when you set your intention. What does that mean? It means *choosing* to walk through chaos into serenity. It means *choosing* to give up the victim role. It means, above all else, being *committed* to walking steadfastly and bravely into the world of possibilities and the unknown. That's the next level of healing, and only you can control that.

The life-altering situation in which you may find yourself is quite possibly your personal wake-up call. It's time to take care of your mind, your heart, your body, and your soul, but now on *your* terms. Although I relied on my family and friends to look out for my best interest when I could not, I was, ultimately, in charge of the breadth and depth of my healing. Only I had the right and responsibility to choose my path to recovery and my companions for the healing journey.

Give yourself permission to think outside the box. Be cautious of well-intentioned family members and friends who may challenge your choice of healing partners and healing options. Most objections come from love, but also from misguided fear.

In truth, we are always divinely guided, so if you find that one course of action doesn't suit you, feel free to change your mind. Be your own best friend. Be the master of your new creation.

Ready to repeat after me? *I am in charge of my healing.* Yes, you are.

A Gentle Rain

I walked in ...
to heal my body,
my cloak of silent protests and fear
wrapped tightly round my heart.

"Let's take a walk," you encouraged,
certain of the journey.
"Are we there yet?" I queried often,
reluctant and impatient.

Holding my hand, you led me
word by word and thought by thought
out of the protection of my cloak,
into the gentle rain.

Stripped of my protests,
awed by the clarity
of the rain-swept path,
my parched soul awakened.

The gentle rain
touched my mind with understanding
and quenched my thirsty soul
with its peace.

Today I am alive,
grateful to the One
who brought you
and the gentle rain into my life.

Written by the author to honor one of her teachers.

Simple Truth Number 6

Your soul has chosen this experience.

Imagine that you are no longer at the mercy of circumstances that are seemingly beyond your control, and that life is the end result of your highest intent, in all instances. That is, in fact, the nature of your reality.
Rasha[10]

Are you riding a roller coaster between feelings of forgiveness and unforgiveness? I was. To get off that ride, I had to rethink and deepen my understanding of victimhood.

I initially absolved the RV driver of his carelessness. Why this generosity of spirit? He certainly didn't mean to hit our vehicle, I reasoned. Surely he was suffering; no one could cause such trauma and not feel deep regret. And realistically, if I didn't forgive him, I would feel anger each time I turned my neck, each time my skull ached, or whenever one of life's pleasures was compromised by my physical condition. Reasons enough to forgive.

---

[10]   Rasha, receiver and transcriber, *Oneness* (Santa Fe, NM, Earthstar Press, 2003).

Later we learned that the state patrol officer who was first on the scene had remarked to my family members that he had never witnessed such lack of remorse as that demonstrated by the RV driver. All feelings of compassion and forgiveness drained from my heart when I heard that, and I was back to square one.

Well-meaning loved ones and friends may share their sympathy by expressing their anger at the guy who did this to you, that terrible disease, or that horrible thing that happened to you. We are conditioned by society to believe things happen *to* us, so blame is our right, and forgiveness is ours to bequeath or withhold. But playing the role of a victim can delay healing.

Early in the recovery process, a dear friend gently suggested that I had brought this incident into my life for a purpose. I was horrified! Why would I do this to myself? Why would I do this to my husband? To my loved ones? My brain blocked out almost five months of tears and pain, but my husband remembered every one of those moments as he cared for me.

Despite an initial resistance to her words, the thought lingered. Books came to my attention to support her suggestion. What was initially a tough concept to wrap my brain around became another doorway to miraculous healing. I asked myself, "What if?"

What if this experience, as Rumi says, had been sent as a guide from beyond?

What if I had orchestrated this experience for my walk into a more conscious life?

What if the collision was essential to my husband's spiritual growth as well?

What if everyone involved in the collision was on a perfect journey, being offered an opportunity to look at life more deeply?

What if believing this simple truth could change my view of the experience, and I could release anger, judgment, and resentment—forever?

Would forgiveness become irrelevant—instantly?

Would living the life as a victim cease to be an option—immediately?

Rather than asking "Why me?", I prayed, "What do I need to learn?" If I did indeed choose this experience at an unconscious level to become fully conscious, I was a willing student. I decided to surrender into this simple truth.

Today, by believing this simple truth, I walk steadfastly in gratitude no matter the outcome or challenge facing me. This can be your gift, too. Try out the possibility and notice how you can let go of blame, anger, and revenge. Aren't these reasons enough to hold this simple truth close to your heart? I think so.

Be brave now and repeat after me: *My soul has chosen this experience.* It has.

Simple Truth Number 7

You are safe.

*A light always appears, even in the densest fog. It
is not our job to know the precise nature of that
light. It is our job to continue to move forward.*
Panache Desai[11]

This simple truth is perhaps the most important truth. Come
along with me on this ride.

I longed for a feeling of safety while feeling tossed by the
winds of life. I longed for a promise of protection, a guarantee
that nothing could ever hurt me like this again. As we
complete our reflections, I now long to offer *you* a knowing[12]
that *everything is always working out for you.* The storminess of
life has exhausted you. You deserve a safe harbor.

---

[11]   Panache Desai, *Discovering Your Soul Signature* (New York, NY,
     Speigel and Grau, 2014).

[12]   Knowing is more than a belief. Belief comes from repetition of a fact
     until the fact is believed or the source of the fact is trusted beyond
     one's own understanding. Knowing comes from the heart, not the
     head. It's a visceral experience.

The collective consciousness of our society buys into the belief that safety comes from an external source—from an insurance policy, a security system, false bravado, a persistent striving, accepting nothing less than winning, and obeying the rules. In truth, it does not and cannot come from any of these sources because the foundation of that mindset is the man-made lie we call fear. And although fear *feels* real, it's simply a chosen perspective. Perspectives are self-made and whimsical.

During my recovery, I used a myriad of external objects and my imagination to give me a sense of protection, gracing me with moments of relief from the confusion and chaos of my circumstances, moments of relief from terror. Uplifting messages pinned all over the rooms in the hospital and at home, religious icons, thoughts of my Grandma protecting me—these were my objects of perceived protection. Yet, the comfort was only temporary, and I wondered why.

The walk into an unconditional knowing that everything is always working out is a walk that involves bravely shedding the perspective of the collective consciousness, testing the waters of surrender and trust, and most of all, befriending and being the guardian of your emotions. It is a singular, authentic walk independent of any other individual, organization, dogma, or religion. I call it a *spiritual* journey because it is a soul-driven and soul-supported process.

Most of our feelings are on autopilot, having been sealed into a box at different stages of life, relegated to the out-of-season closet to avoid embarrassment or self-loathing if brought to light. Well into middle age, I treated any negative feeling as the enemy, a reminder of my imperfection. No wonder I didn't want to look too closely! When I was further encouraged to define *where* in my body I felt an emotion, I thought, "Why would I want to do that?"

Emotion = e(nergy) in motion. Positive emotions raise the vibration of that energy within and keep it healthy. Negative emotions, especially when stuffed, swallowed, or blocked, cause disease. When you are feeling good, bask! Feel the good feeling in your body—for as long as you possibly can. When a negative emotion arises, you can move it through your body quickly by simply observing it and blessing it. Consciously relax your body, breathe in and out with attention to the breath, and say "I love you" to whatever is arising. When you do this, you allow it to run its course and move on through and out of your body. No harm done—to anyone!

Ever the willing student, I committed to being a quiet, faithful screener and guardian of every good as well as every unsettling emotion: Is this thought serving me? Does this perspective make me feel good? Can I reframe it to feel better? It is a singular, authentic, creative, and empowering process, completely within your control. As you practice the art of befriending every emotion, you are poised for taking control of your life and achieving an intimate relationship with I Am Safe.

Ready to try another *what if*?

What if there are two parts of you: the Physical and the Nonphysical. Let's say the Physical You is the body or that aspect of self that is visible to the eyes and embodies the mind, personality, and emotions. What if this body is a small but vital aspect of a much greater, unseen Nonphysical You that some call God or soul? What if this Nonphysical You is an immense ocean of swirling energy or Divine Consciousness[13] of which we are an aspect?

What if the Physical You knows fear, but the greater Nonphysical You embodies "all is well"? What if this greater Non-physical You is your most precious, kind, and gentle friend? Imagine having a sidekick who is devoted to only *you*, and is *always and only* focused on *you*. It is sourced in Love. It *is* Love. What if, whether you believe it or not, It has your back? What if you could *always* rely on your greater Nonphysical You to steer you for your greatest good? Wouldn't that be something? Our brains are simply not equipped to handle the breadth, depth, or specifics of this incomprehensible benevolence.

But let's go one step further. What if every emotion is a guidepost to knowing what your greater Nonphysical You knows about each situation, steering you into a healthy choice at a moment's notice? Imagine a powerful ally like *that*. Nothing and no one can control you when you learn to befriend your emotions.

If you're ready to choose this good-feeling perspective, then, with deep gratitude and trust, repeat after me: *I am Safe.* You truly are.

---

[13] Some use the name God or Source or Universe. Name it as you wish.

Epilogue

I experienced incredible fear, unfathomable pain, and overwhelming uncertainty. Yet today a sense of unshakeable trust envelops my mind and heart as I've come to embody these seven simple truths. Things going on in the world no longer throw me off kilter. I know that everything is always working out for me—and for the world as well. That's an amazing state of grace.

When I finally realized that no one could take this journey of physical healing as well as growth into consciousness for me, I committed myself to a discipline of self-discovery and change. The result is that I no longer fear the lessons I continue to bring into my life.

And now I send you on your way with this wish, taken from *The Road Back to You* by Jan Morgan Cron:

May you recognize in your life the presence, power, and light of your soul. May you realize that you are never alone, that your soul in its brightness and belonging connects you intimately with the rhythm of the universe. May you have respect for your individuality and difference. May you realize that the shape of your soul is unique, that you have a special destiny here, that behind the façade of your life there is something beautiful and eternal happening.

To inspire your practice of meditation ...

*Your energy field is your treasure. Protect it with all
that you are, all that you do, and all that you have.*
Rasha[14]

I became aware of the simple truths through the spoken and
written words shared by friends and teachers. I did not embody
the value of each, however, until I heeded some advice that
was initially very uncomfortable for me: I learned to meditate.

If you already take time out of your day to quiet your mind,
you're ahead of the game. If meditating leaves you feeling as
though you are in unknown and uncomfortable territory, I
understand completely. The most difficult parts of starting a
meditation practice are honoring the importance of quieting
your mind, and making time to do so regularly.

Before the collision, meditation seemed disconnected
from my life, an unnecessary burden. Pushed to the edge
by the aftermath of the impact, I relented to the persistent
encouragement of a friend and started a practice. At first I
thought I had to sit a certain way, hum a certain sound, stare at
a certain object, and achieve a certain outcome. When a friend

---

14   Rasha, receiver and transcriber, *Oneness* (Santa Fe, NM, Earthstar
      Press, 2003).

suggested that it didn't have to be complicated, I decided to be gentle with myself and make my own rules.

The three key elements to a practice are:

1. *Desire.* The practice begins with the intention to live from a deeper awareness, allowing the soul to take center stage for a brief period of time every day.
2. *Discipline.* Daily practice is most beneficial. Fifteen minutes and a quiet place is all it takes. Within a short period of time, you will long for the space and the peace it brings.
3. *Patience.* It is not unusual to feel impatient in the beginning. You will want to get up, quit, and work on your to-do list. If you keep at it, however, you will notice all aspects of your life changing for the better.

There is no wrong way to meditate, but the breath *is* our Life Force, so I encourage a practice that incorporates focused, rhythmic breathing. Sit in a yoga pose, or sit in a chair, but keep an erect spine so the energy can flow unimpeded throughout your body. You can internally speak an affirming phrase as you breathe in and again as you breathe out, or you can breathe to a guided meditation. You can breathe in and out while you stare at a flame, or breathe deeply while you walk in nature. Regardless of the method you choose, know that very moment of *focused breathing* shuts down the mind chatter, internalizes the shifts in your awareness, and gives the cells of the body time and space to heal.

To inspire your healing journey ...

The Gift of Change by Marianne Williamson. HarperCollins, New York, 2004. ISBN 0060816112

A guide to viewing any change or experience as a gift.

The Law of Attraction by Esther and Jerry Hicks. Hay House, California, 2006. ISBN 1401917593

A jump-start to a journey out of victimhood.

Oneness received and transcribed by Rasha. Earthstar Press, Santa Fe, NM, 2003. ISBN0965900312

An affirmation of conscious transformation and truth.

Living the Wisdom of the Tao by Wayne C. Dyer, PhD. Hay House, Inc, California, 2008. ISBN 1401921493

A gentle, inspiring translation of ancient wisdom.

Friendship with God – An Uncommon Dialogue by Neale Diamond Walsch. G. P. Putnam's Sons, New York, NY, 1999. ISBN 0425189848

A joyful walk and talk with a precious friend.

The Hidden Messages in Water by Marasu Emoto. Beyond Words Publishing, Hillsboro, OR, 2004. ISBN 0743289803

> A stunning experiment about the power of every word.

Discovering Your Soul Signature by Panache Desai. Speigel and Grau, New York, NY, 2014. ISBN 97801812995589

> A gentle "33-day path to purpose, passion, & joy."

Life After Life by Raymond Moody, Jr, MD. HarperSanFrancisco, 1975, 2001. ISBN 0062517392

> Comforting words about death, dying, and ultimately, living.

Way of the Peaceful Warrior – A Book That Changes Lives by Dan Millman. H. J. Kramer, Inc. Tiburon, CA, 1984. ISBN 0915811006

> A tale that does indeed change one's perspective about life.

The Four Agreements by Don Miguel Ruiz. Amber-Allen Publishing, San Rafael, CA, 1997. ISBN 1878424319

> A staple for anyone's intentional, conscious journey into a well-lived, peaceful life.

Whatever Arises, Love That by Matt Kahn. Sounds True, Boulder, CO, 2016. ISBN 7981622035304

> A method of self-care that begins with self love.

The Divine Arsonist: A Tale of Awakening by Jacob Nordby. Awakened Life Publications, 2012. ISBN 101469964082

> A surprising tale of transformation.

Complementary Healing Modalities

All the talent in the world won't heal you. Practitioners are *facilitators* eager to open doors to your well-being, but your *intention* holds the key to their assistance. If you are willing, healing will happen.

When choosing a healing practitioner, I look for the qualities of gentleness, respect, and experience. I seek people who challenge my thinking and broaden my awareness. I work with those who understand the roll of facilitator, and who honor me as the healer.

The principle behind most alternative healing systems is that energy is the Life Force that travels throughout the body on pathways called meridians. As we go through life, this energy can become blocked due to physical, emotional, or chemical trauma; disease; exhaustion; suppressed emotions; stress; fear; surgery; or accident. When the flow of energy is blocked, the body is primed for manifesting illness. Reactivating the movement of this energy (called *qi* or *chi* in Chinese medicine and Taoist philosophy or *prana* in Indian medicine and Hindu philosophy) aids the cells' natural ability to communicate and balance. The effects can be immediate or may occur over time. Many of these therapies are grounded in ancient Tibetan or Chinese history, dating as far back as 5,000 years.

I've presented these modalities alphabetically, not in order of effectiveness, preference, or importance. I am not a doctor or medical practitioner. In no way am I endorsing any system or methodology. Neither am I assuring healing, because that is completely up to you.

Acupressure – A type of massage that applies finger pressure on specific acupuncture therapy sites to promote the flow of energy and, therefore, healing and wellness.

Acupuncture – The Chinese medical procedure of treating illnesses and injuries by inserting needles at specific sites on the body. The process also can provide local anesthesia.

Aromatherapy – The therapeutic use of plant-derived, aromatic essential oils to promote physical and psychological well-being.

Bach flower remedies – Flower essences prepared as liquid remedies and directed at a specific emotional state. Can be purchased at most health food stores. www. bachcentre.com

Body work – Therapies and techniques in complementary medicine that involve touching or manipulating the body: massage, Reiki, Rolfing, the Feldenkrais Method, craniosacral therapy, shiatsu, Zero Balancing, and qigong, to name a few.

Chelation therapy – A medical procedure that involves the administration of chelating agents to remove heavy metals from the body.

Chiropractic – A drug-free system of complementary medicine based on the diagnosis and manipulative treatment of mechanical disorders of the musculoskeletal system, especially the spine, promoting optimum nerve impulse transmission between brain and all the organs and systems. (Blair Technique and Network Chiropractic require minimal adjusting.)

Craniosacral therapy – A noninvasive, hands-on system of complementary medicine intended to detect and alleviate imbalances in the central nervous system. Practitioners may apply light touches to a patient's cranium, spine, and pelvis.

Homeopathy – A system for treating physical and psychological disease based upon the administration of minute dilutions of specific remedies that, in a healthy person, would produce symptoms of disease.

Hypnotherapy, color therapy, sound therapy, and neuro-linguistic programming – Various complementary modalities used to identify and transform unconscious patterns and energy blocks in organs as well as in the subconscious.

Kinesiology – The science of body movement. Applied kinesiology involves the testing of muscles to identify structural, chemical and/or emotional imbalances in the body.

Matrix Repatterning – Manual therapy that restores structural balance, eliminates pain, and improves overall health by resolving a problem at the cellular and molecular levels.

Movement therapies – Tai chi, qigong, and yoga are three familiar therapies that strengthen, calm, and center energy.

Naturopathy – A system of alternative medicine based on the theory that diseases can be successfully treated or prevented without the use of drugs by using techniques such as control of diet, exercise, and massage.

Neuro Emotional Technique (NET): A mind-body technique that improves many behavioral and physical conditions by finding and removing neurological imbalances related to unresolved stress.

Reflexology – A system of massage used to relieve tension and treat illness based on the theory that there are reflex points on the hands, feet, and head linked to every part of the body.

About the Author

Kathy was born in Wisconsin but has called the mountains of Colorado her home for the last fifty years. She is a wife, mother, grandmother, sister, friend, former nun, and spiritual sojourner who has enjoyed writing; creating pottery; quilting; outdoor activities; golf; and traveling by motorcycle, automobile, and RV.

Kathy has been a seeker of truth all her life. Because religious community life failed to satisfy her yearning for connection with her Source or provide answers to her deepest questions, she disengaged from any religious affiliation, and then struggled in the ensuring years to find meaningful, spiritual understanding and guidance. The physical challenges she faced in the collision in 2002 presented not only the impetus but also the time to take her search to a deeper level, becoming the greatest gift of her life. The simple truths emerged to sustain her and give purpose and clarity to the next season of her life.

Kathy's writing flows from a lifetime of compassionate service, including volunteer work in hospice, hospital, and numerous other settings. *Repeat After Me* is her first published book and shares her walk into physical, emotional, and spiritual healing.

Reader Reviews

Kathy Adis reminds us that the journey toward body, mind, and spirit wellness is not a passive following, but rather the soulful choosing of daily practices that support life. Beth Owens, Dipl. Ac., L.Ac.

Kathy discovered meaning and purpose in her ordeal, and as an act of generosity, she shares her journey with us. Beyond the healing of her book, Kathy's ability to trust herself and the benevolence of life freed her. Her story redirects our energy toward our own growth and higher purpose. Marlin D. Hoover, M.Div., PhD

Storytelling is one of Kathy Adis's greatest strengths—displayed here in spades. Whether you've lost a loved one to cancer, your home to a hurricane, or your perspective on day-to-day life, this book will guide and recenter you. Gripped by the first few pages, you wont be able to put it down—you'll come away inspired to live with a sense of purpose and renewal. Cindy Skalicky, CEO, On Point Communications, LLC.

Out of a horrible experience has come a powerful story of understanding, forgiveness, love, and hope. No matter our

journey, Repeat After Me *inspires us to take our next step toward wholeness.* Don Johnson, Attorney

Must read for anyone who as ever asked, Why me? Aaron E. Skalicky, PhD, Clinical Psychologist

When someone walks back from the face of death with a message, we all need to listen. Linda Dean, Medical Intuitive

Repeat After Me *offers a beautifully simple message filled with hope and how-to steps for all of us wishing to recover from any sort of life-changing event. Not only does Kathy Adis invite us to accompany her on this journey of recovery, but she provides a wonderful road map to self-empowerment that helps clear the path for each of us as well.* Karon Buckner Scott, Personal and Business Development Clairvoyant

In a time of personal tumult from a devastating injury, Repeat After Me *made its way to my bedside and never left. In the bleakest of time, it was the most important tool that guided me on my journey to physical and transformational healing.* Mary Gauden Beardslee, HTR, Horticultural Therapist

Printed in the United States
By Bookmasters